DATE DUE

OCT 8 1986		MAY 2 8 1999	
2 9 NOV 1986		MAR 1 0 2004	
AP - 6 87			
DEC 9 1987		JAN 0 3 2016	
MAY 24 1988			
NOV 6 1989			
JAN 6 1990			
JAN 2 3 1992			
APR 1 2 1996			
MAY 1 - 1996			
MAY 2 1 1996	MAR 1 2 1999		

SOME MAJOR EVENTS IN WORLD WAR II

THE EUROPEAN THEATER

1939 SEPTEMBER—Germany invades Poland; Great Britain, France, Australia, & New Zealand declare war on Germany; Battle of the Atlantic begins. NOVEMBER—Russia invades Finland.

1940 APRIL—Germany invades Denmark & Norway. MAY—Germany invades Belgium, Luxembourg, & The Netherlands; British forces retreat to Dunkirk and escape to England. JUNE—Italy declares war on Britain & France; France surrenders to Germany. JULY—Battle of Britain begins. SEPTEMBER—Italy invades Egypt; Germany, Italy, & Japan form the Axis countries. OCTOBER—Italy invades Greece. NOVEMBER—Battle of Britain over. DECEMBER—Britain attacks Italy in North Africa.

1941 JANUARY—Allies take Tobruk. FEBRUARY—Rommel arrives at Tripoli. APRIL—Germany invades Greece & Yugoslavia. JUNE—Allies are in Syria; Germany invades Russia. JULY—Russia joins Allies. AUGUST—Germans capture Kiev. OCTOBER—Germany reaches Moscow. DECEMBER—Germans retreat from Moscow; Japan attacks Pearl Harbor; United States enters war against Axis nations.

1942 MAY—first British bomber attack on Cologne. JUNE—Germans take Tobruk. SEPTEMBER—Battle of Stalingrad begins. OCTOBER—Battle of El Alamein begins. NOVEMBER—Allies recapture Tobruk; Russians counterattack at Stalingrad.

1943 JANUARY—Allies take Tripoli. FEBRUARY—German troops at Stalingrad surrender. APRIL—revolt of Warsaw Ghetto Jews begins. MAY—German and Italian resistance in North Africa is over; their troops surrender in Tunisia; Warsaw Ghetto revolt is put down by Germany. JULY—allies invade Sicily; Mussolini put in prison. SEPTEMBER—Allies land in Italy; Italians surrender; Germans occupy Rome; Mussolini rescued by Germany. OCTOBER—Allies capture Naples; Italy declares war on Germany. NOVEMBER—Russians recapture Kiev.

1944 JANUARY—Allies land at Anzio. JUNE—Rome falls to Allies; Allies land in Normandy (D-Day). JULY—assassination attempt on Hitler fails. AUGUST—Allies land in southern France. SEPTEMBER—Brussels freed. OCTOBER—Athens liberated. DECEMBER—Battle of the Bulge.

1945 JANUARY—Russians free Warsaw. FEBRUARY—Dresden bombed. APRIL—Americans take Belsen and Buchenwald concentration camps; Russians free Vienna; Russians take over Berlin; Mussolini killed; Hitler commits suicide. MAY—Germany surrenders; Goering captured.

THE PACIFIC THEATER

1940 SEPTEMBER—Japan joins Axis nations Germany & Italy.

1941 APRIL—Russia & Japan sign neutrality pact. DECEMBER—Japanese launch attacks against Pearl Harbor, Hong Kong, the Philippines, & Malaya; United States and Allied nations declare war on Japan; China declares war on Japan, Germany, & Italy; Japan takes over Guam, Wake Island, & Hong Kong; Japan attacks Burma.

1942 JANUARY—Japan takes over Manila; Japan invades Dutch East Indies. FEBRUARY—Japan takes over Singapore; Battle of the Java Sea. APRIL—Japanese overrun Bataan. MAY—Japan takes Mandalay; Allied forces in Philippines surrender to Japan; Japan takes Corregidor; Battle of the Coral Sea. JUNE—Battle of Midway; Japan occupies Aleutian Islands. AUGUST—United States invades Guadalcanal in the Solomon Islands.

1943 FEBRUARY—Guadalcanal taken by U.S. Marines. MARCH—Japanese begin to retreat in China. APRIL—Yamamoto shot down by U.S. Air Force. MAY—U.S. troops take Aleutian Islands back from Japan. JUNE—Allied troops land in New Guinea. NOVEMBER—U.S. Marines invade Bougainville & Tarawa.

1944 FEBRUARY—Truk liberated. JUNE—Saipan attacked by United States. JULY—battle for Guam begins. OCTOBER—U.S. troops invade Philippines; Battle of Leyte Gulf won by Allies.

1945 JANUARY—Luzon taken; Burma Road won back. MARCH—Iwo Jima freed. APRIL—Okinawa attacked by U.S. troops; President Franklin Roosevelt dies; Harry S. Truman becomes president. JUNE—United States takes Okinawa. AUGUST—atomic bomb dropped on Hiroshima; Russia declares war on Japan; atomic bomb dropped on Nagasaki. SEPTEMBER—Japan surrenders.

WORLD AT WAR

Hitler Youth

WORLD AT WAR

Hitler Youth

By R. Conrad Stein

Consultant:
Professor Robert L. Messer, Ph.D.
Department of History
University of Illinois, Chicago

CHILDRENS PRESS ®

CHICAGO

Late in April, 1945, only a few days before the end of the war in Europe, Adolf Hitler emerged from his bunker below the ruined Reich Chancellery (above) to award medals to a group of boys.

j943.086 (1)

FRONTISPIECE:
Hitler waves to a throng of children gathered in Berlin for a vast meeting of Hitler Youth held on May Day, 1934.

Library of Congress Cataloging in Publication Data

Stein, R. Conrad.
  Hitler youth.

  (World at war)
  Includes index.
  Summary: Describes the origin and growth of the Nazi youth organization known as Hitler Jugend, its rigorous testing and training of German boys and girls, and its use in World War II.
  1. Hitler-Jugend—Juvenile literature.
2. Germany— Politics and government—1933–1945— Juvenile literature. [1. Hitler Youth.
2. Germany—Politics and government—1933–1945] I. Title. II. Series.
DD253.5.S74 1985   943.086   85-11370
ISBN 0-516-04763-9

PICTURE CREDITS:
NATIONAL ARCHIVES: Cover, pages 11, 15, 19, 20, 23 (top and bottom right), 25, 26, 31, 33 (top and bottom right), 42, 44, 46
UPI: Pages 4, 8 16, 23 (bottom left), 37, 40
U.S. ARMY PHOTOGRAPH: Page 6
WIDE WORLD PHOTOS: Pages 12, 13, 18, 22, 24, 27, 28, 30, 33 (bottom left), 34, 36, 39, 41

COVER PHOTO:
A typical member of the Hitler Youth

PROJECT EDITOR:
Joan Downing

CREATIVE DIRECTOR:
Margrit Fiddle

Late in April, 1945, the ruined city of Berlin lay in the shadow of huge Russian guns. Heavy Red Army tanks rumbled through its suburbs. Once-mighty Germany was on the verge of a disastrous defeat. Yet, in the rubble of Berlin, a strange ceremony took place. Adolf Hitler emerged from the bunker that had been his home for weeks to award medals to a group of boys. Upon seeing Hitler, the boys snapped to attention. Some of them were only twelve years old. The leader of the group later said, "Everyone was shocked at [Hitler's] appearance. He walked with a stoop. His hands trembled. But it was surprising how much willpower and determination still radiated from this man."

Among the boys who received medals for bravery in the last days before the defeat of Germany was the twelve-year-old with whom Hitler is shaking hands.

Hitler shook hands with the boys, pinned medals on some of their shirts, and said words of encouragement. Then he returned to his bunker and the boys marched proudly back to battle. Many would die for a cause that already was long lost.

Historians sometimes call the youth of Nazi Germany the "duped generation." All their lives they had heard and read endless lines of propaganda: blond-haired, blue-eyed "Aryan" people were superior to all others; Jews were the enemies of Germany; to die for Germany was an honor; cowardice in battle was an unthinkable disgrace. The propaganda had turned many of Germany's young people into unthinking, unquestioning robots.

The Nazis achieved power in 1933. In a speech that year Adolf Hitler said, "When an opponent declares 'I will not come over to your side,' I calmly say, 'Your child already belongs to us. What are you? You will pass on. Your descendants, however, now stand in the new camp. In a short time they will know nothing but this new community.' "

Germany had long been a country where boys and girls joined youth clubs. Most of the churches had youth clubs. Even political parties sponsored boys' clubs and girls' clubs. In 1922, the infant Nazi party started its own youth organization. It was called the *Hitler Jugend* (Hitler Youth).

At first, few young people joined the Hitler Youth. Most of the members were children of faithful Nazi party workers. In 1932, enrollment stood at about a hundred thousand. That was a very small number compared with the ten million boys and girls who belonged to other organizations.

When the Nazis gained power, Hitler appointed a man named Baldur von Schirach to head the Hitler Youth. Schirach had listened to a Hitler speech when he was eighteen, and was under the Fuehrer's (leader's) spell forever after. He even wrote rambling poems praising Hitler and calling him "this genius grazing the stars." Curiously, Schirach was American on

Hitler (left) and Youth Leader of the German Reich Baldur
von Schirach (center) inspect a formation of the Hitler Youth.

his mother's side. His mother's ancestors
included a Civil War hero and two signers of
the Declaration of Independence. Schirach was
in his early twenties when he was appointed
Youth Leader, but he could have passed for
seventeen. His boyish looks were important. A
major Hitler Youth principle was "Youth
Leading Youth."

At Hitler Youth camp training sessions, boys were drilled on Nazi ideology.

With Schirach in command, the Hitler Youth became the most powerful youth movement in Germany. To achieve power, Schirach used an old Nazi tactic—force. With about fifty muscular teenaged boys, Schirach marched to the office of the German Youth Associations. They invaded the office and took files containing the names of millions of young people who belonged to rival youth organizations. Using those files, Schirach began a hard-sell campaign to sign up new members for the Hitler Youth. Still, the Hitler Youth was not open to everyone. Jews, Gypsies, and other "non-Aryans" were excluded from membership.

Marching Hitler Youth in the streets of Nuremberg celebrated Reichs Party Day on September 1, 1933.

Not satisfied with simply selling their own youth movement, the Nazis began outlawing other youth clubs. Among them was the Catholic Youth Association, one of the largest clubs in Germany. With more and more clubs banned, boys and girls joined the Hitler Youth simply because they had nowhere else to go. By the end of 1938, Hitler Youth membership had zoomed to more than seven million.

Finally, the Nazis issued an order compelling all young people to join the Hitler Youth: "All of the German youth in the Reich is organized within the Hitler Youth. The German youth . . . shall be educated physically, intellectually, and morally in the spirit of National Socialism. . . through the Hitler Youth." Parents could be punished if they failed to enroll their children in Hitler Youth chapters.

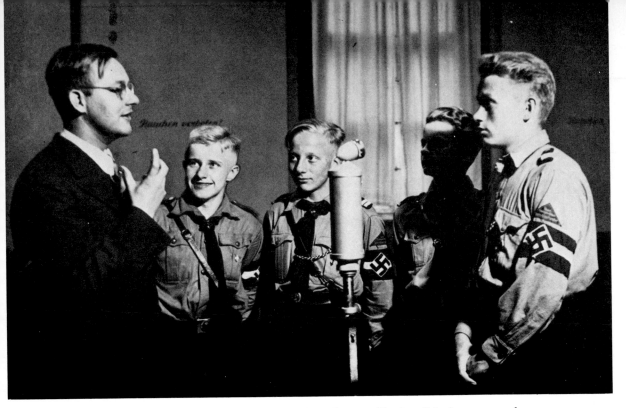

Members of the Hitler Youth prepare to broadcast a Nazi political propaganda message to the young people of Germany.

When membership in the Hitler Youth became compulsory, political propaganda began to deluge the young members. Adolf Hitler had given a great deal of thought to the uses of propaganda and the way it should be spread. In 1923, while serving a prison term, he had written a book called *Mein Kampf* (My Struggle). It is a confusing, rambling book that is difficult to read. But about the use of propaganda the book is quite clear. Hitler said, "Propaganda must confine itself to a very few points and repeat them endlessly."

Under the Nazis, members of the Hitler Youth had to memorize slogans,
take oaths, and sing patriotic songs.

Under the Nazis, members of the Hitler Youth had to memorize slogans, take oaths, and sing patriotic songs. Sometimes what the German children were made to repeat in classrooms and in youth meetings sounded strangely like prayers. In the city of Cologne, boys and girls stood and recited these lines every day before lunch:

Fuehrer, my Fuehrer, bequeathed to me by the
    Lord,
Protect and preserve me as long as I live!
Thou hast rescued Germany from deepest
    distress,
I thank thee today for my daily bread,
Abide thou long with me, forsake me not,
Fuehrer, my Fuehrer, my faith and my life!
    Heil, my Fuehrer!

Typical members of the Hitler Youth give the Nazi salute at a 1935 rally.

To further influence young people, the Nazis seized control of the German school system. All teachers had to take an oath promising "to be loyal and obedient to Adolf Hitler." Anyone who refused to teach according to Nazi principles was fired. A high party official named Wilhelm Frick even wrote an order as to how classroom periods should begin: "At the beginning of each lesson the teacher goes in front of the class, which is standing, and greets it by raising his arm and with the words 'Heil Hitler!' The class returns the salute by raising their right arms and with the words 'Heil Hitler!' "

Nazi official Wilhelm Frick (left) ordered that all German classroom periods should begin with the Nazi salute accompanied by the words "Heil Hitler!" ("Long live Hitler!").

Classroom lessons became crude attempts to prove Nazi theories. In history, the teachers talked about age-old problems Germany had had with its neighbors. But the teachers gave only the German side to those problems. Geography books spoke about the German need for *lebensraum* (living space.) In biology, students learned how to recognize Aryan features. A "true" Aryan had a long, narrow face, blue eyes, and blond hair. Some instructors even used calipers to measure the width of each student's nose. A flat, thick nose was a non-Aryan feature.

Hitler Youth libraries like this one were filled with Nazi-approved books.

The Nazi leaders considered books for young readers to be especially important. Each Hitler Youth chapter had its own library with shelves stacked with Nazi-approved books. Many were stories of events that took place during World War I. During that war, men lived and died in the mud and blood of trenches. But Hitler Youth books portrayed World War I battles as glorious adventures. In a book for teenagers called *The Battle of Tannenberg*, a German soldier named Otto dreams of winning the prestigious medal called the Iron Cross: "A Russian soldier tried to bar the infiltrator's way, but Otto's bayonet slid gratingly between the Russian's ribs, so that he collapsed groaning. There it lay before him, simple and distinguished, his dream's desire, the Iron Cross."

Physical education was the most important part of a German youth's training. About education for young people, Hitler once wrote, "Scholarly and scientific training take last place. . . . A man of small intellectual attainment, but physically healthy, is more valuable to the national community than an educated weakling." Hitler also said that the youth of Germany must become "swift as the greyhound, tough as leather, and hard as Krupp steel."

A Hitler Youth group hikes to its rugged mountain camping area in the Bavarian Alps.

In the Hitler Youth, boys, especially, sweated through long hours of muscle-building activity. They went on long hikes. They participated in gymnastics. They learned how to camp in rugged mountain country during grueling weather. Hitler Youth groups were usually divided into platoons. The leaders encouraged competition between platoons to determine which could hike farthest, run most swiftly, and set up tents the fastest. A particularly successful platoon might reap the ultimate reward—a visit from Hitler himself. After one such visit, a youth wrote, "A holy shiver ran down our spines."

Intensive physical training at
Hitler Youth camps was
intended to produce a race
of superb physical specimens.

Sixty thousand members of the Hitler Youth and the League of German Girls listen to a speech by Adolf Hitler during the 1936 party rally in the Nuremberg sports stadium.

Every September the Nazi party held a huge celebration in a sports stadium in the city of Nuremberg. The celebrations featured events organized by Propaganda Minister Joseph Goebbels. These events included marching bands, a torchlight parade, a display of army weapons, and, of course, a rousing speech by Adolf Hitler. Always the Hitler Youth played an important part in these shows. Long ranks of boys and girls marched into the stadium. The youngsters gave the audience a dazzling

Hitler Youth members applaud during the 1935 Nuremberg rally.

display of gymnastics. Then they recited one of their slogans in thundering unison: "Your name, my Fuehrer, is the happiness of youth; your name, my Fuehrer, is for us everlasting life."

The extravaganzas at Nuremberg served to remind the people that though they had once been a defeated nation, Hitler had led them to unity and pride. "Germans began to hold their heads up again," said a schoolgirl named Melita Maschmann. "At last Germany was no longer the plaything of her enemies. . . . I was obsessed by the vision of a greater German Empire."

Uniformed members of the League of German Girls gather for a songfest.

The girls' branch of the Hitler youth was called the *Bund Deutscher Mädchen* (League of German Girls). Like the boys, they wore uniforms, hiked and camped, and practiced gymnastics. But the Nazis believed in an old German saying that a woman's life should be limited to the three K's—*Kirche, Kinder,* and *Küche* (church, children, and kitchen.) The girls were told they must have healthy bodies, but only so they could grow up and bear many healthy children. It was not until late in the war that women and girls were called upon to work in factories.

These enthusiastic drum-and-bugle-corps members belonged to the youngest class of the Hitler Youth.

The boys' Hitler Youth was divided into three classes. From the ages of six to ten, boys were in the *Pimpf* class. At ten, they were given a series of tests. These included a long jump of at least 2.75 meters, a 60-meter dash to be run in less than twelve seconds, an all-day hike, and the recitation of all verses of the Nazi marching song, the *Horst Wessel Lied*.

Members of a Hitler Youth color guard march through an arch at a castle in Quedlinburg in July, 1936.

Boys who passed the tests became members of the *Jungvolk* (young people). They remained *Jungvolk* until the age of fourteen. Then they took more physical and mental tests before being allowed to graduate into the Hitler Youth proper. The tests might include feats of bravery or resourcefulness. In some platoons, each boy would be taken on a long motorcycle ride down a country road. At twilight, he would be dropped off, alone, and told to find his way back to the base camp before daybreak. Boys remained in the Hitler Youth until the age of eighteen. At eighteen, they either entered the National Labor Service or went into the army.

Boys entering the regular Hitler Youth took an oath as part of a dramatic ceremony. Hundreds of fourteen-year-olds gathered, usually on a sports field. Then, with bugles blaring and drums rolling, they sang the Hitler Youth anthem: "Forward, forward sound the fanfares. Forward, forward, youth knows no dangers." Finally they recited the oath of allegiance:

> I promise
> In the Hitler Youth
> To do my duty
> At all times
> In love and faithfulness
> To the Fuehrer
> So help me God.

Ranks of Hitler Youth spell out *"Wir Gehoeren Dir"* ("We Belong to You") during a massive 1939 May Day celebration held at the Berlin Olympic Stadium.

While passing from one Hitler Youth class to the next, each boy carried a performance book. It was like a report card. In the book, instructors wrote the boy's scores on physical fitness drills and tests on Nazi ideology. The highest achievers were sent to what were called Adolf Hitler Schools. There they were trained in leadership and subjected to even more propaganda. Finally they were returned to the Hitler Youth as platoon leaders. This was in agreement with the Hitler Youth principle of "Youth Leading Youth."

Hitler making a propaganda speech to the youth of Berlin on May Day, 1934

In order to attend an Adolf Hitler School, a boy had to leave home for several months whether his parents wanted him to or not. Hitler Youth member H. W. Koch was ordered to an Adolf Hitler School. His mother protested, but "the headmaster's reply was, 'My dear lady, you had better adjust your ideas. Your son is not your personal property. . . . He is on loan to you, but he is the property of the German people. To object to his name being put forward for an elite school is tantamount to insulting the Fuehrer.'"

Some German young people rebelled against the Hitler Youth. They skipped meetings and encouraged others to do the same. A few youth gangs even formed within the chapters. But these rebellions were short-lived. The Hitler Youth could arrest its own members and hold them in jail on a diet of bread and water. Young people who were especially rebellious had to answer to the Nazi court system. There they could be sent to prison for long terms or even put to death.

By the late 1930s, new branches of the Hitler Youth were formed. A boy could join the Marine Hitler Youth and go on training cruises with the German navy. In the Air Hitler Youth, boys built model planes and studied books on flying. All branches of the Hitler Youth increased their training in rifle shooting. One youth leader said, "We wish to reach the point where the gun rests as securely as the pen in the hand of the boy."

Exuberant Hitler Youth boys (left) had a rousing good time at a 1939 youth festival at Hermann Goering Stadium in Breslau.

During more serious moments, the boys were trained in rifle shooting (below left) and aeronautics (below). Military training was intensified as Hitler brought Europe closer to war.

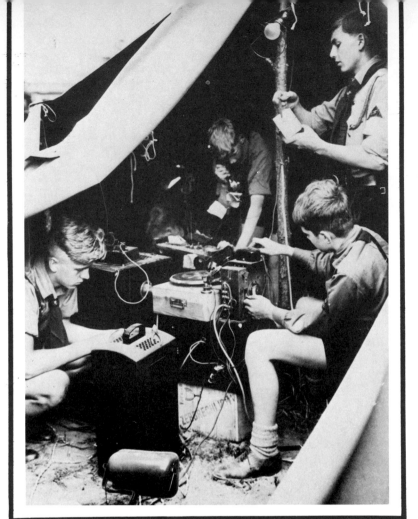

These members
of the Hitler Youth
were learning
to operate
airfield loudspeakers.

Soon thousands of young men in the ranks of
the German army were graduates of the Hitler
Youth. They had been marching since they
were ten years old. They knew how to live
out-of-doors. Almost all of them longed to see
combat, for they had grown up reading that
war is a glorious adventure. Like the heroes in
their books, they were determined to fight
bravely and win a chest full of medals.

On September 1, 1939, German tanks roared into Poland, and Europe exploded into war.

Many Hitler Youth members wanted to join the army immediately. "Why can't I become a soldier now?" asked Harald Juhnke, who was ten years old and a member of the *Jungvolk*. "The Nazis had convinced us that the whole world threatened us, and I wanted to defend the fatherland." Hitler Youth member H. W. Koch wrote, "Throughout the war incidents occurred time and again of a member of the *Jungvolk* faking his birth certificate by a year or so to be accepted [into the army]."

But the Nazis would not permit boys to enter the army. At least, not during the early years of the war.

By the time Adolf Hitler started World War II by invading Poland in 1939, the young people of Nazi Germany were the healthiest in Europe.

The world was soon in awe of the tough young soldiers of Germany. In France, writer William L. Shirer reported on a battle between German soldiers and the British: "The young in the Third Reich were growing up to have strong and healthy bodies. . . . I thought of that later, in the May days of 1940, when along the road between Aachen and Brussels one saw the contrast between the German soldiers, bronzed and clean-cut from a youth spent in the sunshine and on an adequate diet, and the first British prisoners (who had just been captured), with their hollow chests, round shoulders, pasty complexions, and bad teeth. . . ."

To help ease the nursing shortage in wartime Germany, teenaged members of the League of German Girls were trained in emergency medical treatment and first aid.

The war widened in 1940 and 1941 as Germany invaded Russia and Hitler declared war on the United States. But the battles seemed like faraway events to most German civilians. Gradually, however, the horror of war pushed closer to home.

Over the radio, Nazi propaganda announcements proclaimed startling victories in Russia. Still, trainloads of horribly wounded men from that front rolled into eastern German towns every day. Helping to care for those wounded were teenaged assistant nurses who were members of the League of German Girls.

A fifteen-year-old named Irma Krueger gave this grisly description of a makeshift hospital set up in her high school: "The wounded were packed into the gymnasium by the hundreds. . . the doctors passed among them selecting the ones they would operate upon first. . . . Thereafter, the doctors would be operating all day long, their rubber boots and aprons bright red with blood, and our school janitor, Herr Schmitz, would be back and forth all the time, carrying sawed-off limbs under his arms to be burned in the school incinerators in the cellar. It was a terrible time."

But the German civilians' biggest wartime shock came from the air.

Hermann Goering headed the German air force. Before the war, he was asked if the German Ruhr Valley would be safe from bombs in the event that war broke out. "The Ruhr will not be subjected to a single bomb," Goering claimed. "If an enemy bomber reaches the Ruhr, my name is not Herman Goering: you can call me Meier."

Hermann Goering (left) was unable to make good his boast that the *Luftwaffe* (air force) would keep Germany safe from enemy bombers.

In August of 1940, a flight of British bombers churned over the night skies of Berlin and bombed the capital city. The raid did little damage, but "Berliners are stunned," wrote William Shirer after the raid. "They did not think that it could ever happen." That air raid was only the beginning of a reign of terror. In the months and years to come, Allied bombers blackened the sky over Germany. For the rest of the war, when bitter German civilians saw Goering's picture in movie newsreels, they muttered the words, "Herr Meier."

As the war progressed, the manpower shortage in Germany became so great that even very young boys were recruited to help man huge antiaircraft guns like this one.

Air defense became a major task for the Hitler Youth. At first, the boys acted as fire fighters and helped clean up rubble after air raids. But by late 1943, German cities were being pounded by an ever-increasing rain of bombs, and most of the adult males were away at fighting fronts. In many areas of Germany, the boys of the Hitler Youth had to help man huge antiaircraft guns. They also operated searchlights that sent long fingers of light probing into the night skies. Operating antiaircraft guns in the midst of falling bombs, the boys quickly discovered, was not the adventure they had read about in their books.

These Hitler Youth members were trained as fire fighters.

Instead, they learned that war was horror, agony, and death. Melita Maschmann wrote this about some youthful antiaircraft helpers: "In a suburb of Berlin I saw a row of dead *Flakhelfer* [antiaircraft gun helpers] lying side by side. An air raid had just ended. The flak position in which these boys served had received several direct hits. . . . I entered a barrack room in which the survivors had gathered. They sat along the wall on the floor turning their white faces distorted by terror toward me. Many cried."

During the last year of the war, boys as young as twelve were fighting Hitler's battles. These fourteen-year-olds in German army uniforms were captured during an Allied advance east of the Rhine River.

By 1944, German soldiers were retreating on all fronts. It was then that the Nazis began letting boys fight their war.

The *Hitler Jugend* division was made up mainly of sixteen- and seventeen-year-olds. The division first saw action at Normandy, France in 1944, when it faced an advancing British unit. The boys of the *Hitler Jugend* division fought with fanatical courage. In combat, they seemed to remember an often-repeated slogan of the Hitler Youth: "We were born to die for Germany." The British soldiers could hardly believe they were fighting teenagers. Writer

Chester Wilmot said the boys "fought with a tenacity and ferocity seldom equaled and never excelled. . . . they sprang at the Allied tanks 'like wolves,' as a British tank commander recalled, 'until we were forced to kill them against our will.' "

"Youth knows no dangers," proclaimed a line in the Hitler Youth anthem. And the members of the *Hitler Jugend* division attacked the enemy as if they were incapable of feeling fear. But enemy power was too great, and the courage of Germany's boys resulted only in appalling casualty lists. By early 1945, the *Hitler Jugend* division, which at one time numbered ten thousand members, had been reduced to six hundred survivors. The elderly German Field Marshal Gerd von Rundstedt, himself a grandfather, said, "It is a pity that this faithful youth is sacrificed in a hopeless situation."

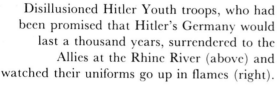

Disillusioned Hitler Youth troops, who had been promised that Hitler's Germany would last a thousand years, surrendered to the Allies at the Rhine River (above) and watched their uniforms go up in flames (right).

As Allied forces rolled into Germany from both east and west, Hitler Youth members were thrown into battle in ever-increasing numbers. Many were only twelve years old. Small and agile, they were given lightweight antitank weapons called *Panzerfaust*. The boys were instructed to creep up on enemy tanks, get within sixty yards of them, and fire. German young people, a generation of believers, tried desperately to carry out their orders. They were slaughtered by the hundreds.

The bitter world of war, however, put doubts in the minds of even the purest believers. As one-time Hitler Youth members grew older and became battle-hardened, many began to question their training. The propaganda drilled into a boy became meaningless when he faced death on a lonely battlefield and dared to ask why. This sense of doubt was painfully expressed in the last letter of a doomed German soldier writing to his sister from a snowy trench at Stalingrad: "Well, now you know that I shall never return. Break it to our parents gently. I am deeply shaken and doubt everything. . . . No one can tell me any longer that men died with the words 'Deutschland' or 'Heil Hitler' on their lips. . . the last word is 'mother' or the name of someone dear, or just a cry for help. I have seen hundreds fall and die already, and many belonged to the Hitler Youth as I did; but all of them, if they still could speak, called for help or shouted a name which could not help them anyway."

The end of the war left Germany in ruins. It also shattered the dreams of survivors of the country's duped generation.

By the end of the war, the few surviving members of Nazi Germany's duped generation had discovered that war was a terrifying, brutal experience—not the glorious adventure they had been led to believe it was.

Index

Page numbers in boldface type indicate illustrations.

Adolf Hitler schools, 30, 31
aeronautics training, 32, **33**
air force, British, 39
air force, German, 38
Air Hitler Youth, 32
anthem, Hitler Youth, 29, 43
antiaircraft gun helpers, 40, **40**, 41
antitank weapons (*Panzerfaust*), 44
army, German, 29, 35, 42, **42**, 43,
   44, **44**, 45, **46**
army, Russian, 7
"Aryan" people, 9, 19
Battle of Tannenberg, The, 21
Berlin, Germany, 7, **30**, 39, 41
books, Nazi-approved, 20
Breslau, Germany, **33**
British air force, 39
British soldiers, 36, 42
Bund Deutscher Mädchen (League of
   German Girls), 26
Catholic Youth Association, 14
Civil War, U.S., 11
Cologne, Germany, 17
Declaration of Independence, U.S.,
   11
drum-and-bugle-corps members, **27**
"duped generation," 9
festival, Hermann Goering Stadium,
   33
fire fighters, 40, **41**
Flakhelfer (antiaircraft gun helpers),
   40, **40**, 41
France, 36, 42
Frick, Wilhelm, 18, **19**
"Fuehrer, my Fuehrer" recitation, 17

German air force, 38
German army, 29, 35, 42, **42**, 43, 44,
   44, 45, **46**
German soldiers, 42, **42**, 43, 44, **44**,
   45, **46**
German Youth Associations, 12
Goebbels, Joseph, 24
Goering, Hermann, 33, 38, 39, **39**
Gypsies, 12
Hermann Goering Stadium, Breslau,
   33
hikes, 22, **22**
Hitler, Adolf, **4**, 7, 8, **8**, 9, 10, **11**,
   15, 18, 21, 22, 24, **31**, 37
Hitler Jugend division, 42, 43
Horst Wessel Lied, 27
Iron Cross medal, 21
Jews, 9, 12
Juhnke, Harald, 35
Jungvolk (young people), 28, 35
Koch, H.W., 31, 35
Krueger, Irma, 38
K's, three, 26
League of German Girls, 26, **26**, 37,
   37
lebensraum (living space), 19
library, Hitler Youth, **20**
loudspeakers, airfield, **34**
Marine Hitler Youth, 32
Maschmann, Melita, 25, 41
May Day celebrations, **4**, **30**, **31**
Mein Kampf (My Struggle), 15
National Labor Service, 29
Nazi party, 10, 14, 18, 30
Nazi salute, **18**, 18
"non-Aryans," 12, 19
Normandy, France 42
Nuremberg, Germany, **13**, 24, **24**,
   25, **25**
nurses, teenaged, 37, **37**

oath of allegiance, 29
Olympic Stadium, Berlin, **30**
Panzerfaust (antitank weapons), 44
performance books, 30
physical education, 21, 22, **22**, **23**, **36**
Pimpf class, 27
Poland, invasion of, 35
propaganda, 9, 15, 30, 37
Quedlinburg, **28**
Red Army, 7
Reich Chancellery, **6**
rifle shooting, 32, **33**
Ruhr Valley, 38
Rundstedt, Gerd von, 43

Russia, invasion of, 37
Russian army, 7
Schirach, Baldur von, 10, 11, **11**, 12
schools, German, 18, 19, 30, 31
Shirer, William L., 36, 39
soldiers, British, 36, 42
soldiers, German, 42, **42**, 43, 44, **44**, 45, **46**
sports stadium, Nuremberg, 24, **24**
Stalingrad, Russia, 45
United States of America, 37
Wilmot, Chester, 43
World War I, 20
youth clubs, German, 10, 14
"Youth Leading Youth," 11, 30

About the Author

Mr. Stein was born and grew up in Chicago. At eighteen he enlisted in the Marine Corps where he served three years. He was a sergeant at discharge. He later received a B.A. in history from the University of Illinois and an M.F.A. from the University of Guanajuato in Mexico.

Although he served in the Marines, Mr. Stein believes that wars are a dreadful waste of human life. He agrees with a statement once uttered by Benjamin Franklin: "There never was a good war or a bad peace." But wars are all too much a part of human history. Mr. Stein hopes that some day there will be no more wars to write about.